CYNEFIN

By the same author

Trace
Alphabet poems
Out of time
Uist waulking song
The art of gardening

Cynefin (Welsh) - (noun) habitat, haunt, place of belonging
- (adjective) accustomed, familiar

CYNEFIN

Mary Robinson

KAILP O T PRESS

First published in 2024
by Kailpot Press,

11 Horsecroft Road
Hemel Hempstead, HP1 1PZ

All rights reserved
© Mary Robinson, 2024

The rights of Mary Robinson to be identified
as the Author of this work has been asserted
in accordance with the Copyright,
Designs and Patents Act 1988.

A CIP record for this book
is available from the British Library

ISBN 978-0-9556860-8-5

Designed and published by Kailpot Press

Front cover photograph © Mary Robinson

www.kailpotpress.co.uk

For my two sons

*Home is the first
and final poem*

Les Murray 'Home Suite'

skylark

pitched
so
high
a
scrap
of
feathers
filters
air
to
unseen
music

CONTENTS

A folk memory of flame	9
Dust	10
Beirut	11
Clay	12
Roofing the world	13
Levels	14
The men	16
The woman	18
The Women	19
Nant Gadwen	21
The mariners	23
Gwydr môr/sea glass	24
Creed	25
Ceremony	26
The boy is silent	27
Reunion II	28
Climbing An Sgurr, Isle of Eigg	30
Hirta *a St Kilda sequence*	31
Wren's nest	34
Red kites at Laurieston	35
Swifts	36
House sparrows	37
The gift	38
Two poems in response to 'Welsh Shepherd'	
i A shepherd speaks	39
ii RS at the writers' workshop	40
Come, says the water	41
Winch	42
Beach cusps	43
Solway	44
Cantre'r Gwaelod	46
What it would be like	47
Black hole	48
Breakthrough	49
Flying to Oslo at the winter solstice	50

Shul	51
My right/write hand	52
(Full) Stop	53
Quotation marks	54
Comma	56
October	57
Saethon	58
October, the hedges	60
Hawthorn tree and ruin	62
Tymor haf bach Mihangel	63
Juniper	64
The pregnant Madonna	65
Woman holding a balance	66
Ginkgo biloba	68
Firestack	69
About cynefin	71
Acknowledgements and thanks	73

A FOLK MEMORY OF FLAME

Once we were familiar with flame –

we tended it as a live creature, we slept
by the flickering shadows on the cave wall

we smelled the peat reek in the crofter's
black house (smooring the fire each night)

it was the place where we kept vigil for birth or death

we knew the craft of setting a fire –
crumpled paper, brittle twigs, a scaffold
of sticks, a log charred from the last fire

the word 'gleed' for the glow in the grate, carrying
coals in a shovel to start the next room's fire

hearth fire, heart fire; proddy rug, inglenook
(where a child and her grandfather sat)

the old prayer 'kindle we pray thee …'

DUST

She is sweeping. A morning task
when light is clearer for weak eyes.
She pulls the brush towards her
as it sighs over clay tiles. She makes
a little mound of dust and ash
(life's daily residues)
and throws it to the wind.

Such particles are not particular –
they colonise cracks between stones,
the site of a demolished factory,
bombed-out flats. Yard walls trail
toadflax, fireweed flames in rubble,
and Aleppo blooms gold.
Every wasteland has a prophecy.

BEIRUT

[For JAS]

The trees would have been greening impossible places
in empty houses and on roof tops
it would have been spring in the city
but on the mountains snow

she would have come
at the same moment you took out your phone
outside the French café just down from the Armenian church
with its pock-marked yellow stone and rose window

she would have been standing behind me
in an ankle-length robe patterned in gold and purple
the hem soiled and frayed by the Beirut streets

strands of ash-grey hair escaped from her scarf
her knuckles poked through her tissue skin
and one eye was clouded over like marble

she would have been carrying a child.

CLAY

Born of movement on the potter's wheel
the vessel balances space and light
sings its own resonance

remember ...
*   before the bowl is broken*
the pitcher shattered at the well

the dog flattens his ears, the cat bolts,
smithereens of slip-glazed ceramic
flung on the midden

wistful shards, silent in earth's darkness
but not still, turned up by coulter and ploughshare
flower-strewn fragments, a smudge of gold rim

in my hand I hold traces of life
of bread shared together
a restless longing, a *hiraeth* for home.

ROOFING THE WORLD

[Dinorwig slate quarry, Llanberis]

They quarried the sea

cascaded
a riptide of galleries
down the rock face

what is left?
white space on a map
an airy atrium open to the sky
a raven's grace

calmness collects
like a still pool
above sheer fall

my fingers trace
initials   dates
my mind plays
with absence

silt finds
a salt-moist bed
in a man's lungs

so many roofs

we sleep under the sea

[It is said that 'Welsh slate roofed the world'. Slate is a sedimentary rock.]

LEVELS

Tide poised between flood and ebb
    land level as harbour stillness
        fields flat as a billiard board's green baize

    and what is the table made of
    but

slate

waterborne to roof the world
tip slates vertical and they're
a fence, slabs wired together, or
a line of gravestones – *er cof am* –
facing the rising sun

whole hillsides quarried away
cartography obliterated
galleries driven deep underground
spoil-tips creaking on storm-nights

slate cleft into sheets, stacked
in wagons like reams of paper
– pages to write on in a village school –
foliated, as if a great stone library were moving
its volumes, page by folio page.

    ★   ★   ★

The toll-booth's boarded up. No one
pays their pence for a paper ticket
marked Rebecca. It's free now to cross
the Cob, Maddocks' great exchange –
land for water, flocks for flood tide, trees for sea bed
    but

see the hoof-prints in mud,
bales rotting, iron gates rusting,
moss sending out spores,
a ditch's green skin pocked by rain

        that thirst for water
    as if the soil still needs to wash
the taste of salt from its mouth.

[*er cof am:* in memory of

Maddocks: William Maddocks (1773 – 1828) built the embankment (the Cob) across the Glaslyn estuary in 1811, resulting in the drainage of a large area of land for agriculture and improved communications. It facilitated the later development of the slate industry and the harbour at Porthmadog.]

THE MEN

[Yr Eifl granite quarry from a photograph]

Great slabs of rock

the quarrymen line up
   not knowing
   what to do
   with their idling hands

waistcoats creased
   from so much bending
buttons chafing
   bound buttonholes
cloth caps
coarse wool jackets
   mended with leather
baggy breeches
   stiff with quarry dust

their faces
   a sprouting of moustaches
   eyes outstaring the camera lens

    proud men, debating men, bettering
        themselves by night at their books

    the dogs
        held still for the photograph

    a foreman squats before
        a heap of broken stone

    and the iron rails
        parallel
        lead out of the picture

    to emptiness

THE WOMAN

What did she bring in a carrier's cart
or the hold of a ship?
a trunk full of linen
    crockery
    a precious picture

what folded memories
    did she leave behind?

Child-bearing   child-raising
her practice and habit of work –
scrubbing   washing   ironing
    flat irons heating
    on an iron black range
tending hens in a back yard coop
cooking and gathering
    berries
    crab apples
    mushrooms
quilting patchwork
not a scrap
wasted

she's found
    in the doorstep's
    hollow tread
the smoothed dip
    in the slate flags
where she stood at the sink

the last layer
    of flowery paper next to rough plaster
a strand of hair
    a trace of her DNA

.

THE WOMEN

[Based on 'The Women' John Charlton 1910]

She was one of the women

who kissed the bairns
in their box beds, left
the eldest in charge
and went into the storm

She was one of the women

blinded with sleet,
who felt their way
through a roar
louder than steam engines
that swallowed their curses

She was one of the women

hands fish-gutted raw
bones stiff with work,
who dragged the lifeboat
three miles along the storm-bound coast
hauled the twisted sinews of rope
pulled together like oxen

She was one of the women

sleeves rolled to the elbow
bodices sodden with sweat
skirts soaked to their shins,
who tasted brine on their lips
their braids loosened to rats' tails
whipping their salt-taut skin
their clogs skidding on stones

She was one of the women

like the pale girl, her cheeks blood-red
with the rope round her shoulders
raising a hand to halt
when she smelt the seaweed,
who paused for breath
at Briar Dene before the steep
descent to the sea, lest the lifeboat
break free and crush them all

She was one of the women

[The painting, in the Laing Art Gallery, Newcastle upon Tyne, commemorates the women who dragged the Cullercoats lifeboat to Briar Dene in a storm on New Year's Day 1861]

NANT GADWEN

Stand and listen – beneath the birdsong
ley-lines of old embankments echo
with the shunt and clank of coupled wagons.
Notice where the lines
break, where a sound
runs on, tumbles
over the cliff into the sea,

and the constant banter of the stream
unspools its cabled water
in a skein of falls,
pouring like molten metal
down to the waves.

There's always something
I don't understand – a tin can
kicked in the mouth of the mine,
the temptation to explore the darkness, the drop
beneath my feet, the way certainties
fall away

in this engineered landscape
where earth's skin has been broken, veins
dissected like the fingers of a glove
peeled inside out.

It attempts erasure
with bluebells and primroses,
the heady scent of gorse,
fleece caught on brambles

but I am not convinced.
It has left its spore on spoil heaps
where nothing grows.
Years accumulate like clouds.
Manganese – I taste the word on my tongue
like salt in the air.

[*Nant Gadwen* (Gwynedd) – site of manganese mining and shipping until 1945]

THE MARINERS

[Capel y Fron cemetery, Nefyn]

Here they have made landfall and while they sleep
soft waves of bluebells and forget-me-nots
wash at their feet. *Y Bedyddwyr* – a religion of water,
of those who go down to the ink-stained sea.
Their graves, garlanded with valerian, lie
higgledy-piggledy tossed on a groundswell
of grass and plantain. After many voyages,
the bitter taste of salt still in their mouths,
they dream in an enchanted meadow
within sight of the sea.

Captains with the names of their ships,
master mariners, widows and infant daughters,
sea-faring sons, those who returned
and those who died far from home.
They rest on the breast of the hill
as if they have just climbed the shrouds
for a better view of the town.

Their haven is amongst the living, looking down
on gables and gardens, lofts and orchards,
on houses with schooners' names. Here at slack water
they are slatily anchored, waiting
until the land falls away and the flood tide rises.
Then they will gather their kin
for one last voyage, slip their slate hawsers
and submit to the ocean's final authority,
bubbles of surf floating like seeds
over the drowned streets.

[*Y Bedyddwyr* – the Baptists]

GWYDR MÔR/SEA GLASS

[*A sea of glass like unto crystal ... mingled with fire* (Revelation 4:6 and 15:2)]

the Atlantic edge
    salt crusting my lips   smell of wrack and kelp

light's glitter playground
    countless   broken   fragments
        endlessly squandered

slivers of goblet   jam jar   cullet

    the sea recycles
        all its flawed
            and bubbled discards

multitudes of mirrors smashed
                          in contempt
    (superstition is nothing
      to eternity)

the sun casts down
    its golden crown
        the swell turns ruby

day tarnishes into night

    and what is faith
        but that we venture forth
            upon a sea of glass?

CREED

How my father trusted the sea. In the days
before plastic he harvested driftwood. The fire
sparked and spat in the grate. Long planks

he saved in the shed. He had been through *the war*,
flown Catalinas and Sunderlands down on the firth.
He knew about shortages, rationing, fending
for oneself, things that *might come in useful*.

The sea is the colour of his uniform.
He quarters the waves, searching for wreckage,
                                                            cast-offs,
someone known unto God.

CEREMONY

My mother,
    who could not swim,
would walk

to the water's edge,
    dip her fingers
in the waves

and touch the sea
    to her forehead
like a blessing.

THE BOY IS SILENT

The boy is silent. He has no words
for the sea's voice. His heart slows,
the swell rises and falls with his breath.

The storm begins as an idea
in the mind of mindlessness. It becomes
a thought, a passion, a fury.

He feels the tide surge in the pulse
of his blood. He stands on the rocks
at the end of the headland

watches each wave's precision
as it shoals to a wall of water, smashes
its green chapel glass to smithereens

then, as an afterthought, draggles
its lacy sleeves on the sand.

REUNION II

Lanes lush with bluebells,
hills emblazoned with yellow gorse.
Ukraine colours. An RAF soundtrack tears the clouds.

The years scatter like mercury. Our unenvisioned
lives have grown old and our children
are adults with children of their own. An acceptance

that there are more years behind us
than ahead; *an absence that is like a presence.*
Another garden – tulips, fringe-cups' creamy bells,

magnolias' pink petals shed like ballet shoes
and in the dusky shadow of a wall
a purple cranesbill – mourning widow.

Next day we park near Cwrt
– early orchids and a bullfinch piping –
and follow the path to the shore. The boat

crosses the Sound, and we in our transitoriness
submit to wind and tide, the water's currents.
There on the island cliff the seabirds

are stacked in their generations; a shadow
passes over – *hebog tramor*, peregrine, *hawk
from over the sea*. The buttercup-coloured catamaran

slips into the Cafn and we embark, tread the track
where islanders and pilgrims have gone before.
Two climb the mountain, see the mainland's

folds and creases, the hollow sea caves which open
under our feet. Two sit in the chapel with its harmonium,
its pulpit's weeping cherubs, its unassuming quiet.
                                                    We gather

for food, walk on through salt air, seal chant,
an oyster-catcher's furious repetition. One sits
and draws while waiting for the boat.

On the last evening, wine, a celebratory meal.
We keep faith with the past. An island
and a garden. Four days, three nights,

a moment out of time, so that we can mourn
a loss which has not yet happened,
rejoice in things not seen.

[Sequel to 'Reunion' p18 *The Art of Gardening* (Flambard 2010)
'an absence that is like a presence' (RS Thomas 'The Absence')]

CLIMBING AN SGURR, ISLE OF EIGG

[In memory KH]

I sit on a rock overlooking the Sound –
down at the pier the ferry embarks,
the car ramp clangs as it folds into the ship,
the tannoy barks in English and Gaelic.
Through the trees I glimpse the white wake
feathering the grey water. Yellow iris,
bluebell, foxglove – how you loved colour –
those shirts, that patchwork waistcoat. My gaze

follows the ship to a speck on the open sea.
I struggle to hold the focus and turn
to climb the Sgurr. You never came here
but how delighted you'd be to see
the pipit's nest I find by the path –
four chicks with gaping orange mouths.

HIRTA

a St Kilda sequence

Lady Grange's cleit

Like a hollow stone skull-capped
with hairy lichen and turf

wheatears and wrens nest in her sockets
and across the angry sea – Flora's birthplace.

1812 Acland's painting of the old houses

A ragged huddle of thatch.
   Pick up
     a stone,
        don't put it down
     until you have found
its place.
    Thicken the walls,
       pack them
     with sand,
   shelter the doors
from winter storms.

1860 Sharbau's map

On Sharbau's map of the new houses
    everything is in order:
the curvature of the village street,
    the croft strips planned and ruled.

Doors open onto the bay,
    corncrakes rasp in the spring,
wind slips over the steps, and damp
    crawls into the stones.

In the school room

Ask: how many pairs of hands for how many hours
did it take to build so many cleits?

but the children are hiding and seeking
in their stone play-houses.

Ordnance Survey map 2008

Not in their right place of course,
but framed in a neat white box on
a spare patch of sea – brown blots
on blue paper. How careless they
look, as if children had dipped their
nibs and flicked ink across the sea.

The flitting

[29 August 1930: HMS Harebell, HMS Dunara Castle]

A Gaelic Bible left in every house
and in the church the page open
at the Book of Exodus –
if it were not true we would want it so.

It was for them an emptying –
not of the place, for what was worth taking
for jobs in forestry with no fulmars?
But they felt in their hearts as if sweet water
had trickled from a bowl
while the islands faded to flecks
on a line between sea and sky.

When did a five year old child, watching
the women who felt the aching
pull as they waved farewell,
notice they had dropped their arms?

teapot   tin trunk   lino   china   jars
lacy mantle-shelf cover   kettle   cooking pot
enamel basin   framed picture of Edwardian lady in
feathered hat and lacy sleeves reading a book   mirror
text The Lord is My Shepherd   medicine bottles
barrels   oil lamp   sheep   the bones of the dead
cats   dogs   chains   rope   oar   trawl-bobbin
Stac Lee   Stac an Armin   Stac Biorach   Borreray
Soay   Dun   Hirta   home

WREN'S NEST

[in memory VMR]

Twigs   bracken   hay   shreds of plastic bag   combings from a
horse's mane   nylon string   wool   lichen   moss   feathers   down

Anything will do
for this pert uptilt fidget of a bird
this beak-and-claw artisan.

His nest is a half-deflated ball
squidged in a cranny
between beam and rafter

almost enclosed except
for that tiny mousehole,
that O – I exclaim – for an entrance.

His spouse finishes the soft furnishings:
over all his other proto-nests
she's chosen this one

in the brown safe dark of my shed.
The way these birds ignore me –
I'd call it defiance

if they weren't so urgent.

RED KITES AT LAURIESTON

A bird's eye view, we say,
    thinking of a map
        or the view from a plane:
a hammer-head
of land jutting into the Irish Sea,
    chains of rivers and lochs,
        roads scrawling
            between towns.

But what their retinas
    receive from below
        is movement – a tractor
    cutting grass, closing in
on the field's bestiary,
    fresh carrion on the tarmac,
        the pick-up truck's
            daily dole of offal.

They gather pell-mell,
    soar and tumble,
        their bellies rufous
    red as squirrel fur.
They feint and parry,
    splayed feathers fold, pleat,
        fan out. They work
            the surface of the air,

rend its walls. Dancers
    of infinite choreography,
        kitten-mewing a suspicion
    there might be something
        more than survival.

SWIFTS

We hear the screams
before we see them –
a chapter of hell's angels
flick-knife wings slashing the air

black-clad dissenters piercing
the street with their keening
risk-taking pitch

smashing the glass hours
of this languid summer afternoon

hooked on speed
they fly straight at us,
veer off at the last moment

keep up, keep up,
we are not one but several
we are not several but one

it is surely a warning – the way
they stake their whole lives
on the globe still working.

HOUSE SPARROWS

August, the year past middle age,
late summer shabbiness getting untidy
at the edges. In the café garden

such gossiping, chattering, tuneless
scrannels, shrill voices calling to each other
and to us. We can scarcely believe

this ubiquity of sparrows,
bucking the trend to decline
and extinction. They flirt and dart, scuttle

between the agapanthus, jostle in hedge queues
for platters of pasties and panini. A waitress
flicks a cloth and sends a feathered cloud

into the air. They swoop, fidget, re-settle,
their joie de vivre infectious. Children hold out
hopeful hands – *this is better than*

Disney! Scarcely-fledged urchins tag along
with their parents – males in dapper grey caps,
females in practical tweedy brownness.

They know nothing of statistics and red lists, only
that some collective ancestral intelligence
took a gamble and threw in its lot with humans.

[Isles of Scilly, August 2022]

THE GIFT

[John Keats and Fanny Brawne]

Chalk spring,
glittering Helicon
plashy with mint and rushes.

There would surely be a naiad
blessing the water as it begins
its rippling journey to the city. The river braids

and tributaries itself,
smells of meadowsweet and water cress,
ambles companionably among sallows
and wheat fields. Downstream

an old corn-mill
harnesses water to make paper,
a flow of continuous milky whiteness
awaiting the consummation of words.

★   ★   ★

At their last parting she gave him a paper-knife,
a talisman against death –

so vivid in her mind that day
when the sun would glitter through the casement,
and he would take his new book in his hand,
slit the unopened pages, hold them to the light,

and see the mark, the river
folded into the paper,
water's calligraphy.

Two poems in response to 'Welsh Shepherd' by R S Thomas

i A SHEPHERD SPEAKS

Why, no, Mr Rogers, Iago Prytherch
never existed. RS – not that I
ever called him that – was a magpie
who pilfered scraps of our lives
to line the nest of his poems.

He was like a child when he came here – everything
was new to him, there were so many things
he didn't understand. Out early,
his leather shoes soaked with dew,

he observed me in the fields,
as he would study a bird
or a hare in the grass,
seeking to grasp our *cynefin*.

He listened as I explained *cynghanedd*,
how to make an *englyn* sing like the music
of curlews on the moor in spring.

He was still rhyming then, his poems as neat and tidy
as his dark suit. But when I saw him standing there,
his back to the rising sun, his eyes to the west,
I knew it would be God he accused, not Iago.

[*cynghanedd* – literally 'harmony'; patterns of stress,
alliteration and rhyme within a line of Welsh poetry
englyn – a frequently-used short form in Welsh poetry]

ii RS AT THE WRITERS' WORKSHOP

Another Prytherch poem, RS?

Verse 1: I'd start *at break of day* if I were you
and cut *behold* – far too archaic for 1949 –
sounds like a hymn or the Bible.
*Hedge-shorn yearling*s – yes, I can see them,
trailing brambles, half their fleeces missing,
and the man with the dog. You bring them alive.
Don't quite understand the last two lines
of that verse – but they sound good.

Verse 2: Of course the man's counting his money –
he can hardly subsist between one mart
and the next. Oh yes, *ravens* – always birds
in your poems. *Swollen fold* is nicely ambiguous.
But *a theme for sentiment* –?
RS, you must drop this habit of telling
not showing. Sonnet form I see – the rhymes heavy
and predictable in my opinion – you need to loosen up a bit.
Not sure about *nimble airs* but that last line's a cracker –
the dawn trimming *his tattered rags with gold*.

['Welsh Shepherd' R S Thomas *Uncollected Poems*, p31
edited by Tony Brown and Jason Walford Davies (Bloodaxe 2013)]

COME, SAYS THE WATER

Come, says the water, this
is your natal element; descend
the ladder in the harbour wall, breathe
the tang of kelp and diesel, step off
from certain ground, let your flesh have faith
in the half-forgotten flow

there might be an otter, or what you thought
was a fishing float is a seal, so curious,
and then another dark head outstaring
your gaze

        and on arrival it's always different
from what you imagined – a farrago
of fish boxes, oil drums, waste skips,
rusting contraptions of the might-come-in-useful,
a crate marked 'Sculpture, with care'.

WINCH

[Ynys Enlli]

A boat bucks and buckles
   against the tide race
      slips round the back of the island
and seeks the nick of the Cafn.

Haul it above the waves,
   wrestle the dead
      weight of a vessel so nimble on water
so lubberly on land.

The winch
   was surety
      for all our landfalls,
embarkations, farewells.

It was authority
   in storms
      as spume and spray lashed
the Narrows.

When it unspooled
   for the last time
      (a boat slipped haplessly
back to the sea)

the winch,
   once cast in sand,
      was stranded ashore.

BEACH CUSPS

An invisible draughtsman
    has left a blueprint on the sand
for our delight, a carnival tracery

of glittering gravel,
    silica sequins,
a frivolous scalloped

symmetry unfurled.
    The sea waits at ebb tide,
its waves lapping gently

after a morning's concentration,
    quietly satisfied at its handiwork
and just a little
               astonished.

SOLWAY

the under-firth
      not swithering
   but thinking

changing its mind,
      making fresh
   (and salt)
      decisions

      the firth's desire path –
        never two slack waters
          (respites from thinking)
the same

     it curates/collates
       its sand and gravel,
every micro-decision
   dependent on the last

    like flocks of knot
      which   lift   flow   turn
        tumble   as if of one mind

       ★   ★   ★

tread the wath
            as the flood recedes
                        and silt slip-drags
        in the water's wake,

                feel the depth
    with your feet,
link arms, brace
            against the current

            how precise the firth
(you want to take sides,
                black or white, right or wrong)
        how imprecise the border

                when the tide turns
                ripples slip into channels,
    haaf-netters peel off the line
as if in a slow motion ceilidh

consider the opposite opinion –
            the racing tide meeting outgoing water,
                the white-edged bore with its surge and roar
        trailing tattered rags of broken surf

thalweg – how the word flows off your tongue
    until it lodges, for a moment, on that final *g*

CANTRE'R GWAELOD

That a girl named Mererid
allowed the well to overflow,
that a drunkard called Sethenyn
left the flood gates open.

It was always someone else's fault.
Shingle spits were dead-end roads
running into the waves. Fishermen
sighted kelp-covered walls.

There is a kingdom under the sea
and the church bells of its fair city
clang beneath the water. After the storm

a drowned forest gasps for air, we find
footprints, fire-cracked flint, a worked blade.

Remember the next flood.

[*Cantre'r Gwaelod* – legendary submerged kingdom in Cardigan Bay]

WHAT IT WOULD BE LIKE

    the long day's smirr lifts   this will not do
  beyond the headland I see   even as I look
  a shimmering pool far out   the pool tarnishes

I wonder what it would be like to sail there

    cut the engines and drift   engines stall
          resting on water   the boat starts to sink
 where light holds its breath   a father
    on the mirror of the sea   with a child in his arms

BLACK HOLE

We speak in metaphors
beginning with a general term
named after an atrocity of war

our algorithms stitch together images
    data's Bayeux Tapestry
we add the language of the body
    at the heart of the Messier 87 Galaxy
and religion
    a halo of dust and gas

a heart-stopping confection
of red and gold
with blackness at its centre

so distant capturing it
is like sighting
a bagel on the moon

on the stage of the event-horizon
there's a cosmic trap door
where light and matter
    all that makes sense of our lives
disappear never to return

Powehi – defined by darkness
haunting
the other side of creation

[Based on press coverage (*The Guardian* 13 April 2019) of the first image of a black hole, named Powehi by Professor Larry Kimura. The name means 'the adorned fathomless dark creation' and is derived from an 18th century Hawaiian creation chant.]

BREAKTHROUGH

When the road to the airport is closed
and forests grow in the tower blocks
someone sends from an illicit transmitter
the earth's last radio broadcast
which is picked up on a planet,
not unlike our own, in another galaxy
millennia away, where sound archaeologists
work back from electro-magnetic waves
and, after many failures, construct
an instrument to play the sound –
a Bach partita – and whisper
This is what their planet was like.

FLYING TO OSLO AT THE WINTER SOLSTICE

There's a garland on the ash-grey clouds,
each water-drop a prism which unbraids
the falling light. Cast free from earth
this rainbow ring's a serpent's sloughed-off
skin, once bejewelled and dazzling,
now a pallid image of itself,
a spectral annulet abandoned
on the cloudscape's clints and grykes.
Our shadowy cross transits the circle
and we fly on, the horizon fading
to a shore we'll never reach. Far below,
the setting sun's last rays pierce
the chambered darkness of a cairn.

SHUL: the spaces in between

As

one listens for a loved one's next breath

wrinkled crevices interpret an aged face

furrows between fingerprints condemn or absolve

a line made by walking is a corridor between grasses

Ruskin lace appears from drawn threads

a traveller glimpses the sea between strangers' houses

night is cleft by day and to walk at night is to read the dark

a river changes its mind about where to make its bed

spiders decipher webbed air trembling between filaments

a hollow in the ground is warm from the body of the hare

so

a scribe   remembering the miracle of the well by the shore

which still issued fresh water at the salt tide's diurnal flood

made between each word a sacred space

a clearing   for imagination's dance

[*Shul*: 'a mark that remains after that which made it has passed by'
Rebecca Solnit *A Field Guide to Getting Lost* (Canongate 2006) p50-51]

MY RIGHT/WRITE HAND

wearing its threadbare apparel
easily torn, scratched by thorns,
a blue bruise bubbling
beneath the surface;
the burn-scar

that darned itself to a circle of skin,
pale and taut as vellum;
skin which makes and remakes
itself repairs, renews, re-creates
as fingers do

ever industrious, ever touching;
my hand is a fan which folds and splays
(that opalescent arc between
finger and thumb),
tanned, blotched, sun-stained

foxed as an old book,
veins exposed like knotted roots;
I lick my fingers, taste salt, oranges,
moorland bilberries cupped to my mouth;
tips translate a language of touch

as, in darkness, I learn
the textures of another's skin;
take my hand
smell the scent at my wrist
hold my pulse until the end of time.

(FULL) STOP

.

a dot of ink before another thought

the land's spot height
music's staccato note

seed   spore   pollen grain
speck of beetle frass on wood

magnified it becomes a teeming city

o

what of the fullness
    the panache
of a doodler's exuberant punctuation

the moon
so bright the trees cast pewter shadows

a pool of stillness in a brimful glass

a bowl's equilibrium of space and light
when the potter's wheel has ceased

the amplitude of many dimensions

even the word contains a full moon
the eye's pupil.

QUOTATION MARKS

Seeing the lights of a car, on a winter's night,
slowly moving down the narrow lane, twin beams

flickering between oak trees, a fox crossing ahead of them
and inside the car two figures surrounded by darkness

except for the dashboard's faint glow on their faces,
I remember driving across the moors with my father

the long distance home on a Friday night after work
and I wonder what those two people are saying and if

I could transcribe it and if it would be in quotation marks. Surely
this is what we want – the exact words, the longing

for even a whisper to voice those precise words. The past
vanishes, all those unrecorded conversations, the way

we cling in memory to a familiar phrase
or that oft-repeated endearment only the family knew.

We treasure each word, like a chipped marble clasped
in a child's hand. The nearest we can get perhaps –

and yet always that slippage between speech
and thought, the inarticulacy of words, the things left unsaid.

These marks, these matching pairs, these twins or quads
are like the curves of an arch or a cruck-framed gable

enclosing another life nesting within, a heart-beat away
from utterance. What difference do they make?

All our follies and foibles, our misunderstandings,
things said in haste, but also our tenderness,

fondness, rejoicings. Do they steal the soul
like an old Daguerrotype, the sitter awkwardly perched

on an elaborate chair draped with brocade?
or are they a keepsake, locks of hair?

I have your words but not your voice.

COMMA

Although he's a jaunty fellow
in his serif beret, he hardly pauses
for breath as he separates
his subordinate clauses.
Compulsive tabulator, avid collector,
clip-boarded bureaucrat –
he can't finish a sentence
without butting in.
Even sans serif, sans hat, reduced
to a stub of punctuation,
he insists on that panda joke.

[*panda joke* – see *Eats, Shoots & Leaves* Lynne Truss (Profile Books 2003)]

OCTOBER

Of course I recognise him – it's that
old zip-up jacket I bought at BHS
for his birthday years ago, scuffed and stained
but just the thing for gardening or a stroll
on this brown October day when, as usual,
he's wearing his flat cap – stiffened with grease
from his scalp – and I know so well the way
he walks, that forward lean from the shoulders
as his stick takes the strain of his dodgy knee,
but I wonder how he got here, so far
from home, and even as I glimpse his face
I know the dead are with us still, manifest
in someone else's clothes, a slant
of autumn light.

SAETHON

I read the ridge like Semitic script from right
to left, tracing its lines of wall and field bank

Saethon
Carneddol
Foel Felin Wynt

fields fore-gone
mute patches of plough-work and harrow
seed-fiddle and scythe

the church
Llanfihangel Bachellaeth
grave manuscripts
scribbles of nettle and thorn

Saethon, calligrapher of weather

a rumour of rain
a whisp
-er of mist

spinning its white-out web

its cataract — Saethon blinded
air-born/airborne raindrops
taunting the rocks

static taut as a bow-string
summit fires stone-cold

I watch
I am watched

Saethon
Carneddol
Foel Felin Wynt

the way I walked with my father

OCTOBER, THE HEDGES

(in memory of my father, JHB)

October, the hedges
      clotted
    with blood-red haws

now on your birthday
      I remember you
barrowing bill-hook and bow-saw,
      cutter and axe
    for a day's work
          which always outgrew you

cutting and thinning,
      threading the thorns,
    staking with ash and oak,
pleaching with hazel

no gloves, the flesh of your hands
    blood-beaded by briars

      stitching enclosure's bloodline –
  five fields, twelve acres
(such fields unhedged by your neighbours)

                    you edged
                              your way round the land
in your Harris tweed jacket
            russet colours of autumn
        woven together
          like a hedge – the warp
          and the weft of it
shaped by your body:
                stretched at the shoulders,
patched and creased
            at the elbows,
and, after fifty years,
                    sleeves frayed at the cuffs

not for you the hack and slash
of the machine-cut flail,
        haemorrhag-
              ing berries on stony ground

you kept the slow quiet ways
                        that always outgrew you.

HAWTHORN TREE AND RUIN

Random seed-spit, opportunist quick,
this squatter has an assured tenure.

Haws ruby red, red carpet red, plush velvet red –
such opulence in a tied cottage.

I stand at the threshold, the land falling away
to the sea, the Skerries light, the Irish ferry.

A threadbare lace-cap hydrangea waves
at what once was a window

as if someone from the past has just called round
to see who's home.

TYMOR HAF BACH MIHANGEL

I walk between sea and sky

choughs chack around rocks

    fire-raven   pyrrhocorax
        their splayed feathers
      rising and falling
          fluttering do-si-do

harebells give themselves to the wind
    gold sparks on gorse

here's tormentil to cheer the spirit
    yarrow to heal our wounds
  late heather's charm against winter

the ash tree, some wind-blown volunteer,
    scant hold against the sky – snapped
  leaves withered to stocking brown –
      gall encrusted, dying

but not ready to go, not yet

    the sea chants
      its heavy slow chorale,
    bides its time.

[*Title:* season of Saint Michael's little summer – around St Michael's Day on 29 September]

JUNIPER

Tousled, rubbing the sleep from its eyes,
waking with a shock to find its companions gone.

It straggles a boundary wall, kicks off a few stones and sprawls
sideways, incapable of deciding between earth or sky.

It plays its own ice music – the sound of wind after glacier,
rocks fracturing, a corvid's bark.

Such a distillation of colours in its dark alembic –
malachite, verdigris, viridian, emerald, sage,
the way a raven's feather sheens from black through blue to green.

But what is its aureate crown – a nest, a lair, or the sear
of an angel's wings? for under such a tree
Elijah might have lain down and slept.

THE PREGNANT MADONNA

[*Madonna del Parto* c.1460 Piero della Francesca]

We whisper, though she's not in church.
She's big with child, bigger too than both
her red and green co-ordinated angels.
She's tiring of her mouth's incessant cravings,
the way nothing smells the same.
She hates her velvet dress – the costly gathered
yards of fashion weigh her down. She rubs
against the nap and feels another kick –
she slips exquisite tiny buttons
from their bonds, reveals her petticoat.

The pregnant leave their offerings
of paper prayers. The childless and the child-lost
give her trinkets, flowers, little sheaves of barley,
longing for their bodies to enshrine a child.
And, though she is so ripe, so fecund,
do those whose wombs are barren think back
through their mothers, women born of women
who endured this time of heaviness
with no angels to swish back a curtain
and proclaim the queen of heaven to the world?

WOMAN HOLDING A BALANCE

[Jan Vermeer c.1664]

It is the ninth month and she is with child.
At mid-day equinoctial light illumines
her face, her right hand, her fingers. The tips

catch the light. Her little finger extends –
making a right angle
with the chain she holds between forefinger

and thumb – light falls along its length,
parallel to the beam of the balance scarcely visible,
a luminous cantle on the edge of darkness

catching the curve of each pan. There in the centre
the fingertips and the balance, the symmetry
of the balance at rest,

the asymmetry of her fingers. Light falls
on her left hand too, steadying her stance at the table.
She leans back, her spine a fulcrum

to counterpoise her body's intricate mechanics
with the weight of the child in her womb,
the child who will be born under the sign of Libra.

To see the balance
she must incline her head, as if,
on hearing distant music, she holds in her mind

the stillness at the end of one movement
in expectation of the first note of the next.
She ignores the mirror on the wall

and looks down at the balance. Her contemplation
and mine as I look at the painting –
her blue jacket, the blue cloth on the table

gold from earth, pearls from water. Light
falls on fur and fabric, refines brown cloth
to gold. Sunlight decorates

the seam of her linen head-dress,
and behind her head a painting, shadowed, unfocussed
except for the pale haloed lozenge of Christ

his arms outstretched, weighing the destiny
of agitated souls. A painting of judgement in a painting
of grace. Birth and death, this life and the next,

stillness and chaos. Why would she weigh the jewels?
Where are the weights to put in one pan
to counter the other? What has been removed

from the nail on the wall? There are no answers –
only the silence at the still centre.
It is the ninth month and she is with child.

GINKGO BILOBA

'A living fossil', you say – once as common here
as oak or ash or those lost elms – a solitary remnant
from the Pleiocene. It's like a little fan,
this leaf you gave me from a far-fetched
ginkgo tree, inhabiting the garden
of an old thatched house in Worcestershire.

A marvel it survived
in some hidden valley, tended by monks
who saw the way biloba enacted yin
and yang; and those hibaku trees, blasted
at Hiroshima, death-defying, keeping faith
with life.

The brittle timber's almost useless –
why grow it, except for beauty's sake?

FIRESTACK

[after artist Julie Brook's *Firestack* installations]

fire
   penned
      in the sea

fire broch   beacon   bastion   summons   warning
sea mark   soul mark   flood tide   *I hold my breath/*
diving   hoping against hope it will be safe   stack   skerry
surge   rake   crests tear along the shore   fray the land
stack cradles fire   how vulnerable to the sea's rough caress
sea breath   fire breath   *my breath*   flames blow
towards land   *my mind empties and fills*

     water rising

fire flares in a stone crucible   ochre   chrome   amber
jet   gold

     flood tide rising

I wait for the inevitable end   *as we all wait*   *knowing*
our own mortality   fire-splintered driftwood   sparks'
counterpoint to breaking waves   tongues of fire
tongue music   wind-forged flame-strung harp
woodsmoke   melting plastic   oil fumes   salt on
my tongue

    first wave flushes over

plucky the fire that keeps burning   smaller now   flame
feathers flickering   waves course to the top of the wall
but not over

    tide rising   darkness falling   water calming

I feel the drag   *the heave*   *the pull of water*   *almost
out of my depth*

    a hard wave

determined   dislodges a stone   stone crack   wall
collapse   flames snuffed out   quenched   drowned
extinguished   steam   smoke   grey-blue will o' the
wisp   fire breaking   stack breaking   water breaking
havoc wreaked   elements dissolved

    waves wash over ruins   dismantle time

beyond the bay   the setting sun's desire path glitters
as if for a fleeting moment I could walk
                              on water

fire
    in the midst
        of the sea

ABOUT *CYNEFIN*

'Cynefin' is one of those notorious words which is untranslatable.

In dictionaries it is often defined as 'habitat' but the English word sounds scientific and detached. It lacks the emotional heft of the Welsh. Cynefin has a sense of belonging, of being rooted in a place – in its people, language, history, geography, ecology, culture, everything that gives the place its individual character.

A better approximation might be Shakespeare's phrase 'a local habitation' – which the poet Norman Nicholson, who wrote extensively about his own cynefin of Millom, used as the title of his 1972 collection. Putting the phrase in its original context in Shakespeare's *A Midsummer Night's Dream* gives it an extra dimension:

> *And as imagination bodies forth*
> *The theme of things unknown, the poet's pen*
> *Turns them to shapes, and gives to airy nothing*
> *A local habitation and a name.*

Cynefin is the product of the mind and the imagination. It is a universal human experience. It is a place of both longing and belonging.

In my collection I explore the cynefin of my local area and that of other people in other places. But there are also poems about those who have lost their cynefin – a refugee in Beirut, a family attempting to escape across the sea, the inhabitants of St Kilda evacuated in 1930. There are ekphrastic poems inspired by art which relates to our cynefin. There are poems about birds whose cynefin is so intimately linked with our own.

Some years ago I met a man who told me how, in the turmoil following the Second World War, he and his family had fled to Western Europe. They feared for their lives and were on the brink of starvation. He showed me the only non-essential item they had carried with them – a leather-bound photograph album, a permanent reminder of the cynefin they had lost.

I was born in Warwickshire and first came to North Wales as a toddler – with three adults, two children and a dog crammed into an old Austin 7. It was the first of many visits in a variety of ancient vehicles which always overheated going over the steep mountain passes between the border and the coast. Since then I have lived in several different places, including 26 years in the north of Cumbria. I have shared my cynefin with the habitats of different people, animals, plants, even rocks and water. I have always returned to Pen Llŷn, spending increasing amounts of time here until I came to live here permanently. Why? Because it is my spiritual home. My answer sounds romantic but it is also true.

In the words of J Glyn Davies' englyn ('Lleyn'), a place where the soul finds peace:

Lle i enaid gael llonydd

ACKNOWLEDGEMENTS AND THANKS

Some of these poems have appeared previously in *Artemis Poetry*, *Comet*, *Envoi*, *The Fenland Reed*, *The High Window*, *London Grip*, *Northwords Now*, *Poetry Birmingham Literary Journal*, *Poetry Scotland*, *Two Ravens* anthology ed. Joy Howard (Grey Hen Press 2024) and in the second *Voices for the Silent* anthology ed. Ronnie Goodyer (Indigo Dreams 2022).

'Beirut' was shortlisted in the 2021 Second Light poetry competition and 'Breakthrough' and 'Red kites' were commended in the 2019 competition. 'RS at the writers' workshop' was highly commended in the 2022 R S Thomas festival poetry competition.

Some of the poems were originally written during a collaboration with Anna Dear.

The epigraph to this collection is taken from the first two lines of 'Home Suite' by Les Murray, *Translations from the Natural World* (Carcanet 1993).

Several people have had early versions inflicted upon them and have offered constructive advice and criticism – you are all appreciated. In particular I owe a debt of gratitude to L. Kiew and the Saturday Group poets, Cumbrian poets, Shirley Nicholson, Rachel Porter and Isobel Thrilling, and to Anna Dear, Juliet Fossey and Alison Locke for also reading the draft of this collection. Thanks to Christine Evans for support and a final read-through. My great encouragers have kept me writing – Kathryn Crosby, Christine Raafat, Anne Thomas, Sylvia Pilling and the late Christopher Pilling.

Finally a huge thank you to Andrew and Peter of Kailpot Press for believing in my work and making this book a reality.